Montessori Materials: English Vocabulary Cards

About

Hello, I am a Native English language and Montessori trained teacher with six years International teaching experience. Feel free to contact me for any collaborations or opportunities. I produce all of the English language learning material myself using high quality images of real life stills. I have first hand experience of teaching in a Montessori classroom, Assistant to Infancy (0-3), Primary (3-6), Elementary (6-12). The vocabulary cards have been used in teaching English language through the Montessori method.

Book content cards

- Adjectives x16
- Animal group names x8
- Art x8
- Birds x8
- Buildings x8
- Cookware x16
- Dinosaurs x8
- Directions x8
- Easter x8

adjectives

adjectives

tall

tall

short

short

young

young

old

old

fat

fat

thin

thin

strong

strong

weak

weak

far

far

near

near

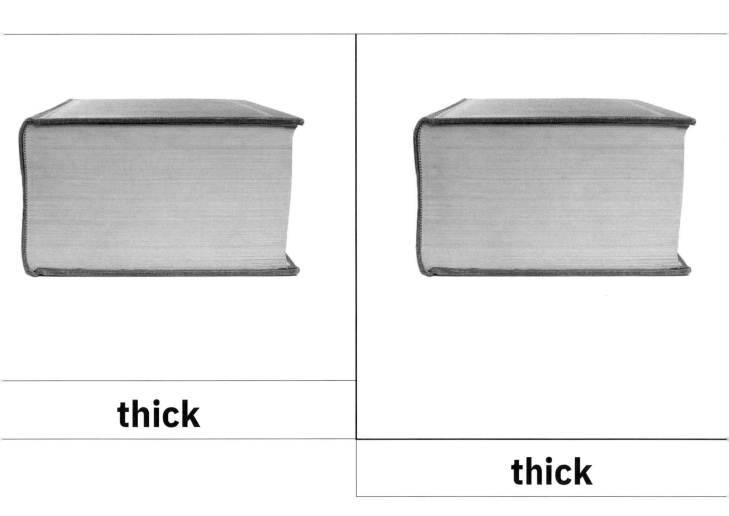

thick

thick

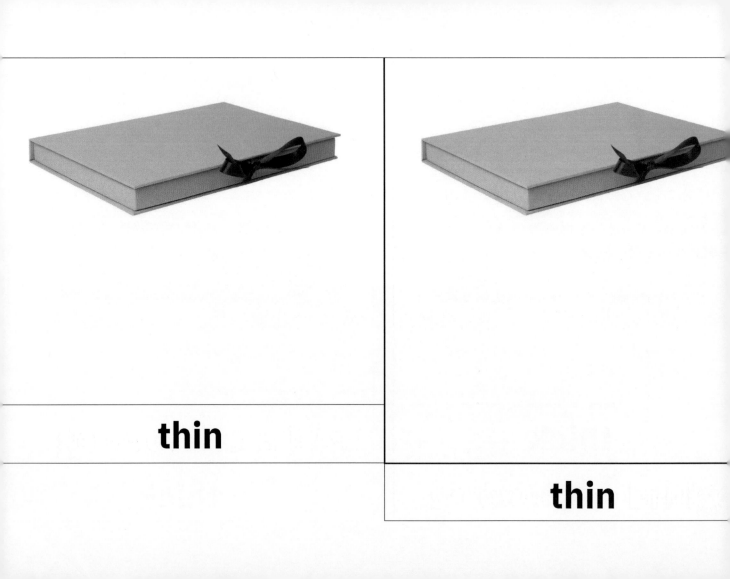

thin

thin

long

long

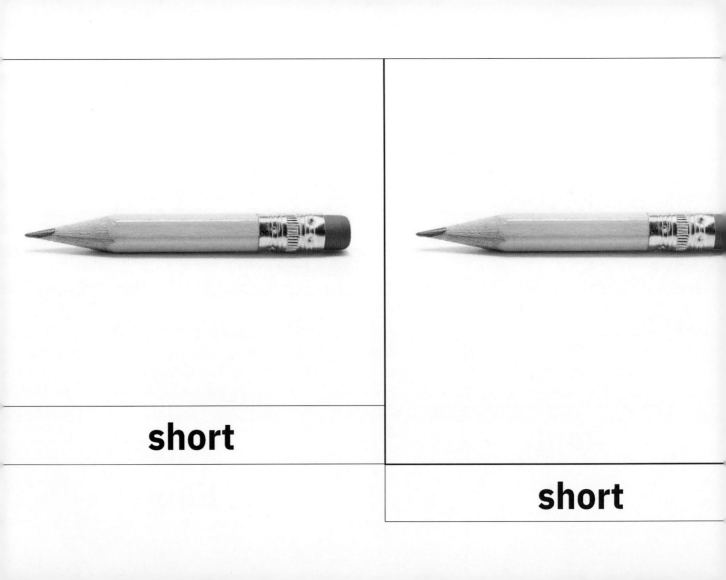

short

short

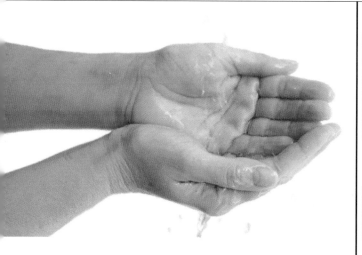

clean

clean

dirty

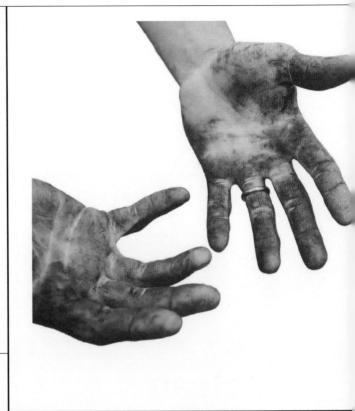

dirty

groups of animals

groups of animals

a pride of lions

a pride of lions

a herd of cattle

a herd of cattle

a colony of ants

a colony of ants

a swarm of bees

a swarm of bees

a flock of seagulls

a flock of seagulls

a pack of wolves

a pack of wolves

a litter of puppies

a litter of puppies

a school of tuna

a school of tuna

art

art

paper

paper

sketchbook

sketchbook

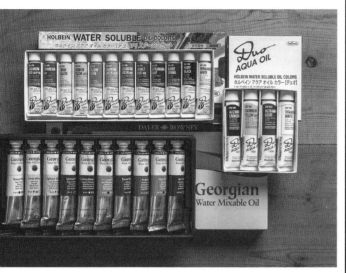

oil paints

oil paints

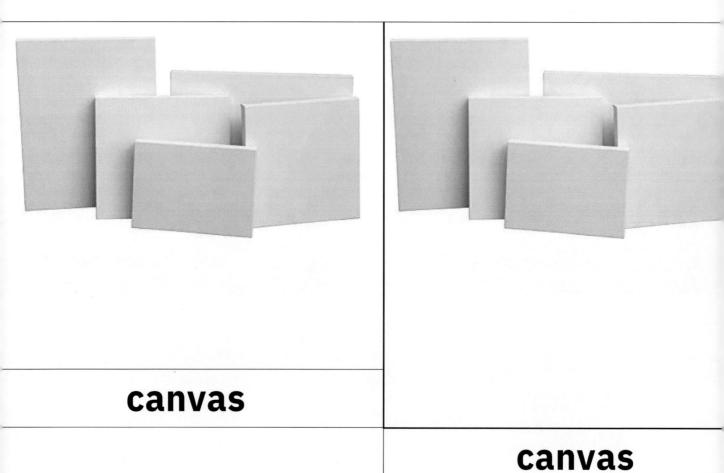

canvas

canvas

charcoal

charcoal

watercolour

watercolour

graphic tablet

graphic tablet

art studio

art studio

birds

birds

duck

duck

robin

robin

dove

dove

owl

owl

eagle

eagle

flamingo

flamingo

vulture

vulture

emu

emu

buildings

buildings

hotel

hotel

skyscraper

skyscraper

house

house

apartment block

apartment block

lighthouse

lighthouse

windmill

windmill

train station

train station

palace

palace

cookware

cookware

pot

pot

colander

colander

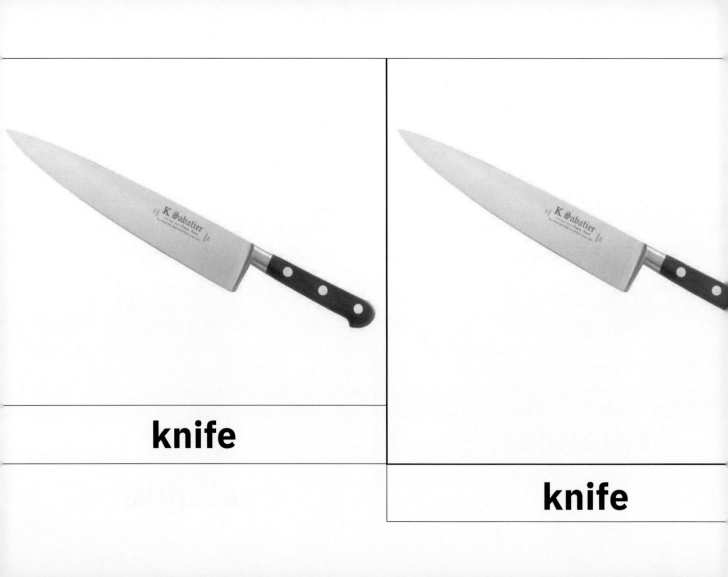

knife

knife

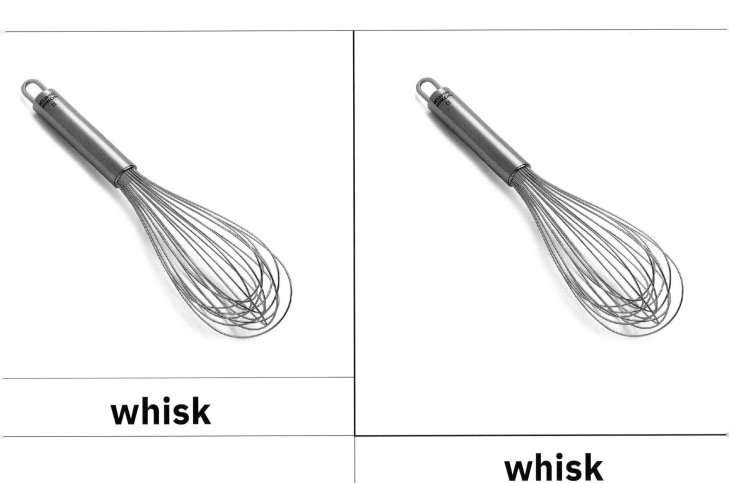

whisk

whisk

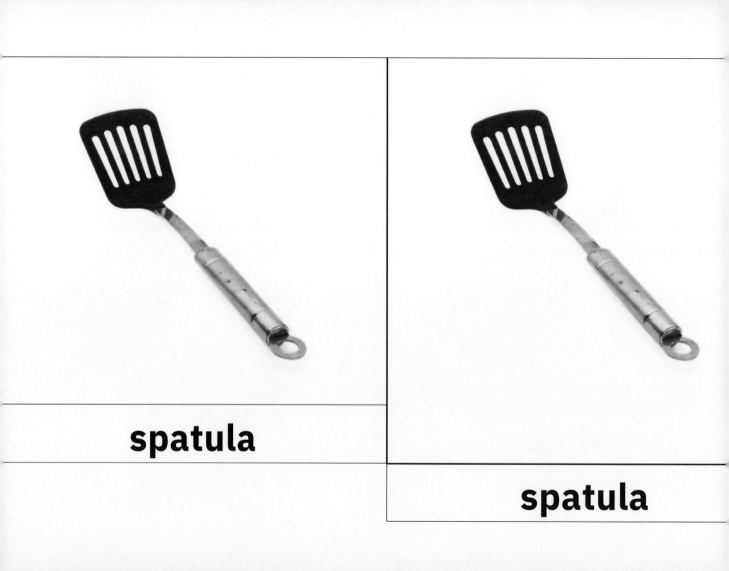

spatula

spatula

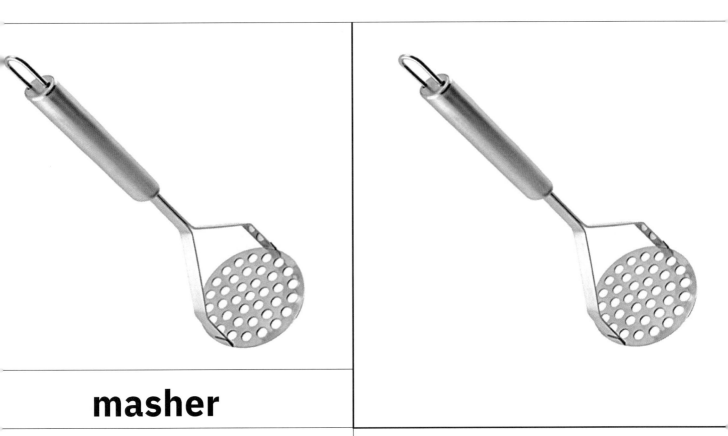

masher

masher

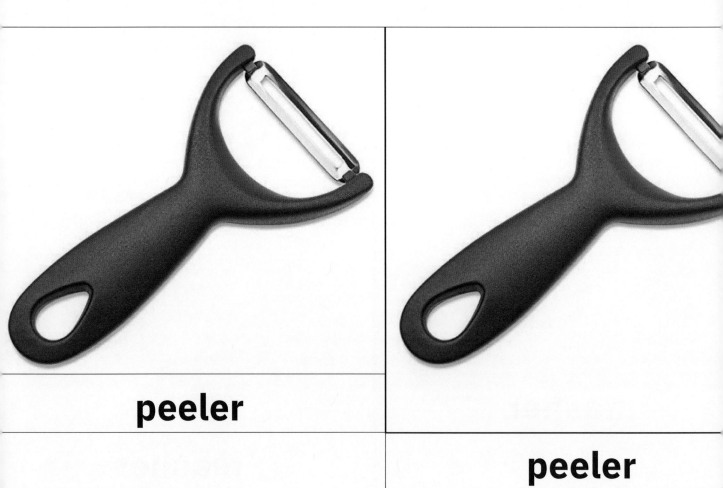

peeler

peeler

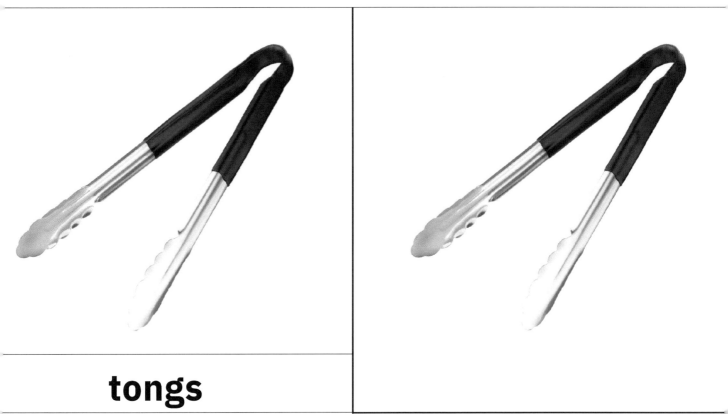

tongs

tongs

frying pan

frying pan

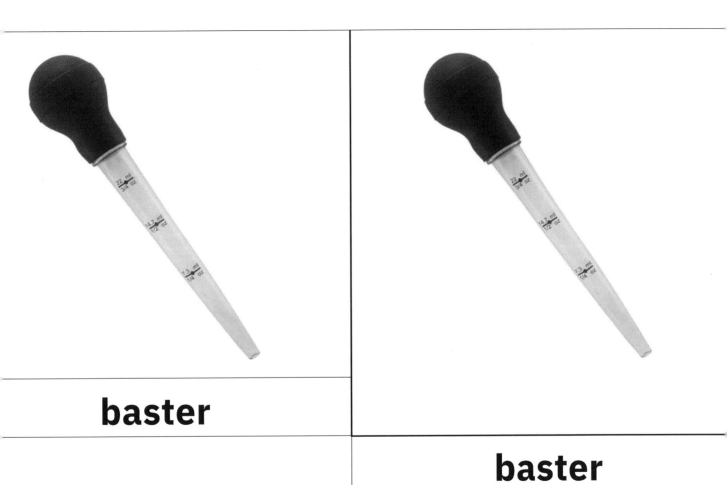

baster

baster

grater

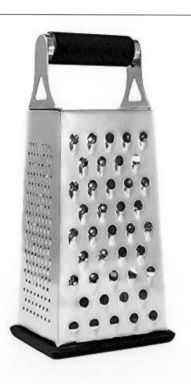

grater

mixing bowl

mixing bowl

measuring cup

measuring cup

scales

scales

pizza wheel

pizza wheel

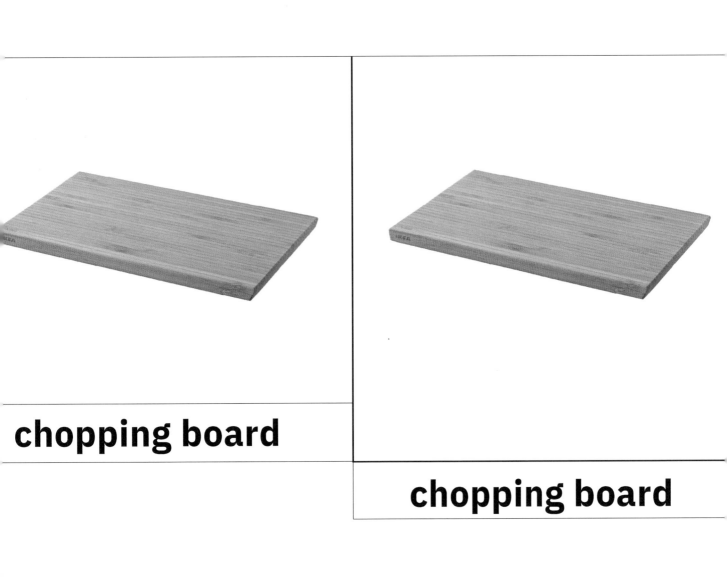

chopping board

chopping board

dinosaurs

dinosaurs

t-rex

t-rex

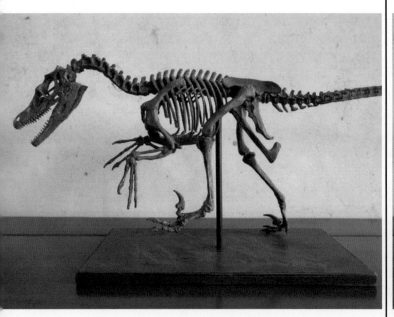

velociraptor

velociraptor

brachiosaurus

brachiosaurus

diplodocus

diplodocus

iguanodon

iguanodon

stegosaurus

stegosaurus

triceratops

triceratops

troodon

troodon

directions

directions

turn left

turn left

turn right

turn right

go straight on

go straight on

roundabout

roundabout

go over the bridge

go over the bridge

read a map

read a map

tunnel

tunnel

zebra crossing

zebra crossing

easter UK

easter UK

easter eggs

easter eggs

chocolate

chocolate

hot cross buns

hot cross buns

basket

basket

bunnies

bunnies

lamb

lamb

chick

chick

nest

nest